BASEBALL IN TULSA

Welcome to one of the greatest baseball cities in America—Tulsa!

BASEBALL IN TULSA

Wayne McCombs

ARCADIA
PUBLISHING

Published by Arcadia Publishing
Charleston, South Carolina

Library of Congress Catalog Card Number: 2003103042

For all general information contact Arcadia Publishing at:
Telephone 843-853-2070
Fax 843-853-0044
E-Mail sales@arcadiapublishing.com
For customer service and orders:
Toll-Free 1-888-313-2665

Visit us on the Internet at www.arcadiapublishing.com

CONTENTS

John A. Ferguson threw out the first pitch at a Tulsa Driller game in 1995
when the ball club held a night in his honor.

DEDICATION

Baseball in Tulsa is dedicated to *Tulsa World* sportswriter John A. Ferguson.

Ferguson covered a variety of sports in his 48 year career with the *World*, from 1952–2000. He died in November 2000 at the age of 75. He was affectionately known as "Fergy" to his friends, a group including just about anyone who ever met him. Ferguson had a positive and energetic attitude about his work, his family, and his friends.

One of my first writing jobs in college was covering high school football for the *Tulsa World*. In those ancient days of the early 1970s, reporters just picked up the telephone and dictated the story back to whoever answered the phone on the sports desk. I prayed it would be Fergy. He would guide me into making my ramblings into complete sentences. Many times I would read the *World* the next day and see my byline on a sports story that was a thousand times better than the one I called in because Fergy would edit it before he turned it in to print. When he would see me he always compliment me.

Ferguson was one of the finest Christian gentlemen I have ever known. I never heard him say a cuss word. I never heard him bad mouth anyone, not even in jest. But he could be one of the funniest people you would ever hope to meet. There was many a night in the press box at Oiler Park or Drillers Stadium that Fergy had the entire crew rolling with laughter.

He dearly loved his wife Frances, son John D. Ferguson, and daughter Jill Wilkis. He also loved baseball. Ferguson could tell a story of watching Lou Gehrig at Yankee Stadium in the 1930s with the same excitement as one about last night's Driller game.

I count it as one of the greatest privileges in my life to have known John A. Ferguson.

INTRODUCTION

Baseball is a special game and Tulsa is a special place for baseball. Since the early Indian Territory days, Tulsa has been a baseball town.

The earliest records show baseball being played in Tulsa in 1893, fourteen years before statehood. Many of the early Tulsa businesses, such as banks and oil companies, hired employees based on their baseball abilities to play for company teams. Early newspaper reports indicate that the city's businesses closed up at 3:30 for 4:00 p.m. games, and employees would go out to root for their co-workers against other company nines.

Minor league baseball in Tulsa is different. A hometown atmosphere surrounds it. You know the feeling… You were in the stands in 1940 rooting for Dizzy Dean to regain that fastball and once again "fog 'em past" the opposing batter. In 1964, you were chanting "go-go-go" when Joe Patterson got on base and was off for another steal of second. You caught a foul ball off the bat of Keith Hernandez in the '73 Little World Series. You were there on that hot Sunday afternoon in July of '78 when Dave Righetti struck out 21. You joined the crowd cheering like crazy when Dan Collier tied the all-time minor league record for consecutive home runs in '97, and you waited out that long rain delay in 2001 to see if Hank Blalock would make history with his second cycle in three games. All Tulsa fans like to think they are part of these players' successes because they cheered them on while playing for Tulsa.

It's like seeing your child or neighborhood youngster grow to be a player on the local high school club and driving in the winning run against the arch rival.

Tulsa baseball fans can call off with pride the names of players they saw wear the Tulsa uniform: Dean, Patterson, Hernandez, Righetti, Collier, Blalock… Spahn, Carlton, Sosa.

Tulsa, with few exceptions, such as during World War I and World War II, has supported professional baseball since 1905. Baseball was close to leaving in 1930, 1960, 1976 and 1979. Support from major league affiliates has at times been lacking, and Tulsa was teased with a chance to regain Triple A status in 1991. Tulsa baseball fans have endured, and Tulsa remains one of the top minor league cities in the country.

Through the pages of this book the reader will see many reasons why Tulsans have loved and continue to love the game of baseball.

ACKNOWLEDGEMENTS

A great deal of gratitude goes to the following people and organizations who provided assistance in the compiling and writing of this book:

FORREST CAMERON, *Greater Tulsa Reporter*—research and photographs

BRIAN CARROLL, Tulsa Drillers—photographs

DALLAS PUBLIC LIBRARY—photographs

JOHN KLEIN, *Tulsa World*—photographs

BARRY LEWIS, *Tulsa World*—research

JUDY McHENRY—photographic artwork

NATIONAL BASEBALL HALL OF FAME—photographs

MIKE PORTER—research and photographs

TULSA WORLD—photographs

GLEN TURNER JR.—research

I would also like to thank my wife, Lea Ann, and my children Mandi, Sam, Susie, and Micah for their love and patience. And above all my Lord and Savior, Jesus Christ.

First Inning

The Early Years

1893–1919

The 1908 Tulsa Oilers of the Oklahoma-Kansas League won Tulsa's first championship with a record of 72-54. Pictured are: 1. Lyons, 2. Long, 3. Speck, 4. R. Gill, 5. Denny, 6. Alford, 7. Saurwein (manager), 8. T.C. Hayden (president), 9. J. Kelly, 10. W. Kelly, 11. Mason, 12. Campbell, 13. Wolverton, 14. J. Gill, and 15. Killillay.

The city of Tulsa was incorporated in 1898. But Tulsa's baseball history can be traced back as far as 1893. "Town Ball" teams were common place among many towns in the Indian Territory. In the late 1890s, with Tulsa's population "growing" to over 1000, a town ball team was formed to play against other cities near Tulsa, such as Bartlesville, Claremore, Sapulpa, and Vinita. The 1897 team was, from left to right: (first row) Sam McBirney, Charles Meadows, and J.H. McBirney; (second row) Arthur Perryman, Vic Prather, Charley Brown, and Roy Funk; (third row) Bob Hall, Frank Murdock (assistant manager), Tom Shackle (manager), John McBride (owner), Ott Boone, Don Hagler, and Hermie Romine (mascot).

Tulsa's early baseball stadiums were little more than wooden stands set up on the edge of town by a cow pasture. Tulsa played in Athletic Park from 1906–1908. It was located on East First Street near Frankfort Avenue.

Jacob Peter "Jake" Beckley managed Tulsa to a sixth-place finish in 1907 in the Oklahoma-Arkansas-Kansas League. Research shows Beckley playing 32 games for the St. Louis Cardinals in 1907. It's presumed he joined the Cardinals when Tulsa's season was finished.

Beckley played in the National League for 20 years, from 1888–1907, mostly with Pittsburgh and Cincinnati. He was a lifetime .308 hitter. Beckley holds the major league record for most games played at first base—2,368. He's the record holder for most putouts at first base in major league history (23,696) and accepted chances at first (25,000). Beckley hit three home runs in a game on September 26, 1897. He managed in the minor leagues for three more seasons and became an umpire in 1913 for the Federal League. He was named to the National Baseball Hall of Fame in 1971. (Photo Courtesy of National Baseball Hall of Fame Library, Cooperstown, NY.)

Tulsa had the nickname of Oilers from 1905–12 and 1919–76. The name Oilers was selected in a contest by fans before the 1905 season. A.M. Fleshman of Tulsa was one of three people to suggest Oilers. Fleshman's entry was selected in a drawing. When Tulsa failed to field a team in 1913, the new owner of the 1914 team decided to adopt the nickname "Producers." Tulsa carried that nickname through the 1917 season. Due to World War I, Tulsa did not field a team in 1918. When Spencer Abbott brought baseball back to Tulsa in 1919, he went back to the Oiler name. Outfielder Clyde Henry (above) led the 1914 Producers, who finished second in the league in batting with a .301 average.

The 1916 Producers won the second half of the split season of the Western Association. Tulsa lost in the playoffs to Denison, Texas. The team was led by a pair of 20 game winners, Geist and Kraft. Pictured are: 1. Moore, 2. Geist, 3. Heatley, 4. Jones, 5. Gleason, 6. Clayton, 7. Kraft, 8. Brandon, 9. J. B. Scott (team owner), 10. Wooley, 11. Murphy, 12. Flowers, 13. Smith, 14. Lamb, 15. Brady, and 16. Stewart

Jesse Joseph "Pop" Haines pitched for the 1919 Oilers. He recorded a 5-9 record in 101 innings. He was sold to Kansas City in June and pitched another 213 innings and won 21 games! In 1920 he reached the majors with the Cardinals and lasted 18 years. Haines won 210 games for the powerful Cardinal clubs of the 1920s and 1930s, pitching in four World Series. He was one of the earliest masters of the knuckleball. Haines was elected to the National Baseball Hall of Fame in 1970.

Spencer Abbott moved his Western League club from Hutchinson, Kansas to Tulsa after the 1918 season. He persuaded the son of M.J. McNulty to convince his father to lease his land at Tenth and Elgin in downtown Tulsa for a baseball park. Short on cash, Abbott sold half his interest in the Oilers to Tulsa oilman Jim Crawford. Abbott went to St. Louis to see Ed Steienger, the contractor who built Sportsman's Park, home of the Browns and Cardinals. That stadium was home to the Cardinals until 1966. Returning with the plans, Abbott had McNulty Park built as a smaller version of Sportsman's in 22 days from February 10 to March 3, 1919. Abbott managed minor league teams from 1903–1947, winning 2,180 games, fifth all-time in minor league history. With Abbott's arrival and the new McNulty Park, Tulsa was about to begin a Western League dynasty.

SECOND INNING

The Roaring Twenties

1920–1929

In 1920, oil was flowing in gushers, making Tulsa the "Oil Capital of the World." And Tulsa baseball was roaring, winning five championships. McNulty Park, patterned after Sportsman's Park in St. Louis, was a hitter's haven. The cozy dimensions were 310 feet to left field, 320 to center field and a mere 274 feet to right field. Tulsa led the league in hitting seven times during the decade and set many team and individual batting marks. The Oilers won 90 games six times.

The 1927 Oilers won 101 games, won the pennant by 10 games, and were Western League champions. Pictured from left to right are: (first row) Otis Brannon, Stewart Bolen, Marty Berghammer (manager), Patterson, and Ed Grimes; (second row) Karl Black, Pete Casey, Guy Sturdy, Naylor, Smithson, George Blaeholder and Walter Beck; (back row) Kress, Joe Munson, Fred Bennett, Porter, and Hayworth. Sitting in front are Jim Crawford (mascot) and Floyd (batboy).

After moving his Hutchinson, Kansas franchise to Tulsa in early 1919, Spencer Abbott was in need of financial backing. After talking with prominent oilmen all night in his hotel room, Abbott was still lacking the needed funds to build a new ballpark. About four o'clock in the morning, Jim Crawford (pictured here) knocked on Abbott's door. After a lengthy discussion, a partnership was formed. For half interest in the team, Crawford built McNulty Park and stocked the team for their first season. In 1921 Abbott sold his share to Crawford, who remained the principal owner through the 1929 season. "Gentleman Jim" was born in County Derby, Ireland, in 1870. His family moved to New York state when he was 14. He served in the Spanish-American War and then moved to Oklahoma in 1913 as director of the Sperry and Crown Oil Companies and figured largely in the Oklahoma oil boom years. In 1920 he was listed as one of the 50 millionaires that lived in Tulsa. His friendship with St. Louis Browns owner Phil Ball helped in getting great players for the Oilers.

16

Lyman Lamb was one of the greatest hitters in Tulsa as well as minor league history. He set the all-time organized baseball record of 100 doubles in a single season (1924). Lamb played third base for the Oilers in 1916, hitting .281. He also played outfield from 1922–1925. He had 224 hits and a .361 average in 1922, 241 hits and a .341 average in 1923, and 261 hits and a .373 average in 1924. Lamb couldn't bring the success he had as a hitter to the dugout and he was fired as Oiler manager in July of 1925, with Tulsa in next to last place. Lamb played for the St. Louis Browns during parts of the 1920 and 1921 seasons.

Karl Black pitched for 20 years in the minors from 1911–1930. He won 110 games for Tulsa from 1922–1927. Black's greatest season was in Tulsa's championship year of 1923, winning 29 games. In his minor league career, Black, whose real last name was Lautenschlager, pitched in 814 games and over 4,400 innings. He won 275 games. The left-hander never made it to the major leagues.

The four powerful hitters pictured in the next photos helped the Tulsa Oilers dominate the Western League in the 1920s. Yank Davis played outfield for Tulsa for five seasons, 1919–1924. He became Tulsa's first league home run champ, with 35 in 1922. He is third on the Tulsa all-time list for home runs in a season with 42 in 1924. Davis led the team in doubles three times, had 240 hits in 1923, and scored 161 runs in 1922.

Joe Munson was a left-handed slugging outfielder on Tulsa's three consecutive championship teams of 1927–29. He led the league in home runs with 32 in 1927, hits, runs scored, and batting average (.385) in 1928, and hits in 1929. He hit three home runs in one game in 1929. Munson played 15 seasons of minor league ball from 1918–1932. Munson, whose real last name was Carlson, played 42 games for the Chicago Cubs in 1925 and 1926.

Guy Sturdy was Tulsa's all-time single season home run champion, hitting 49 blasts in 1926. A left-handed hitting first baseman, Sturdy hit .353 and scored 163 runs in 1926. He also hit .346 in 1925 and .347 in 1927. An injury in 1928 cut down his power stroke. He played in over 2,100 career minor league games from 1920–1940 with a career batting average of .322. Sturdy played parts of the 1927-28 seasons with the St. Louis Browns.

Fred Bennett was an outfielder on back-to-back 1927 and 1928 champions. He hammered the ball for a .385 mark in 1927 and batted .371 in 1928. He hit 35 home runs in 1928. He played minor league baseball from 1924–1939 with an amazing .343 career average. Bennett played seven games for the Browns in 1928 and 32 for the Pittsburgh Pirates in 1931.

For years major league clubs would leave spring training camps and play exhibition games against minor league teams on their way north to start the season. On April 8, 1924, the Chicago Cubs played Tulsa at McNulty Park. Before the game some members of the Cubs and Oilers get together for a friendly photograph. The Cubs must have turned nasty after this photo was taken as they pounded Oiler pitching for 28 hits, 10 of them home runs, in routing the Oilers 25-8!

Hard throwing George Blaeholder won 80 games from 1924–1927 for Tulsa. He won 27 games in 1926 and his 26 wins in 1927 led the league. He pitched in the majors for 11 season, mostly with the St. Louis Browns, winning 104 games. Blaeholder is credited with inventing the pitch now called the slider.

Marty Berghammer played infield in the majors from 1911–1915. He came to Tulsa in July of 1925 when manager Lyman Lamb was fired. Berghammer led the Oilers to championships in 1927 and 1928. He took the Milwaukee Brewers job in the American Association in July of 1929. (Tulsa also won the championship in 1929.) Berghammer won 373 career games, the most by any Tulsa manager until Bobby Jones broke the record in 1998.

Jack Lelivelt managed Tulsa for three record-setting seasons (1922–24), winning 297 games. From 1909–1914 he played first base in the American League for Washington, New York and Cleveland. He turned to managing in 1920. He gained fame as the Los Angeles Angels' manager from 1929–1936, averaging over 100 wins a season for the Pacific Coast League team. In 1934 he won 137 games and lost only 50. In his minor league managing career (1920–1940) he won 1,861 games, 17th on the all-time minor league games won list.

THIRD INNING

Triumph During the Depression

1930–1939

Tulsa's baseball fortunes mirrored the nation's economy in the 1930s. The Oilers lost their lease on McNulty Park after the 1929 season. The city, county, owner Jim Crawford, and St. Louis Browns officials couldn't come to an agreement for a new stadium near Twenty-first and Trenton. The Western League transferred the franchise to Topeka, and Oiler owner Crawford died in the early part of 1930. Tulsa was without professional baseball in 1930 and 1931. But as the nation rebounded so did Tulsa baseball. The Oilers joined the Texas League in 1933 and had great battles with teams from Oklahoma City, Dallas, Houston, and Ft. Worth for the next 25 years. The 1936 Oilers hit the jackpot. After finishing the regular season in third place, Tulsa defeated Houston and Dallas for the Texas League crown. Then Tulsa blew away Birmingham of the Southern League in four straight games for the Dixie Series title.

The 1936 Oilers from left to right are: (seated) George Milstead, Jack Mealey, Marty McManus, manager; William Jackson and Irving Stein; (kneeling) Harold Patchett, Tony York, George Jansco, Ivan Crawford and Bob Allaire; (standing) Murray Howell, Stan Schino, Bernie Cobb, Ed Selway, Max Thomas, and Newell Kimball.

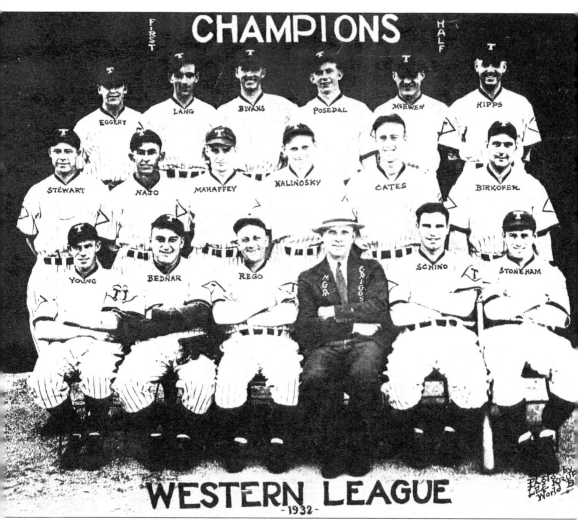

A new ball park was built on the fairgrounds and the Oilers returned for one last season in the Western League. Art Griggs moved his Wichita franchise to town to bring professional baseball to the Oil Capital. Tulsa won the first-half championship and tied Oklahoma City in the second half. The Oilers defeated Oklahoma City four games to none for the Western League crown, their fourth in a row and sixth in 12 seasons in the league. The 1932 champions won 98 games and lost 48. Pictured from left to right are: (first row) Floyd Young, Andy Bednar, Tony Rego, Art Griggs (manager), Stan Schino, and John Stoneham; (second row) Stuffy Stewart, Leo Najo, Roy Mahaffey, Tony Malinosky, Larry Cates, and Ralph Birkofer; (third row) Elmer Eggert, Marty Lang, Jim Bivin, Bill Posedel, McEwen, and Hipps.

Andy Bednar had a fantastic pitching record of 22–4 for the 1932 champions. He led the league in wins and winning percentage (.846).

The batting leader on the great 1932 team was left-hand hitting outfielder John Stoneham. He led the champs in hits, home runs, and triples (20). He hit for a .352 batting average and knocked in 135 runs. Only one other player in Tulsa baseball history hit more than 20 triples in one season—Alex Hooks with 24 in 1934. Stoneham played the next two seasons with Tulsa, playing 304 consecutive games, not missing an inning of play! Stoneham played 14 years in the minors (1928–1941) hitting for a career .317 average. In 1933 he played 10 games for the Chicago White Sox, hitting one big league homer, in Yankee Stadium.

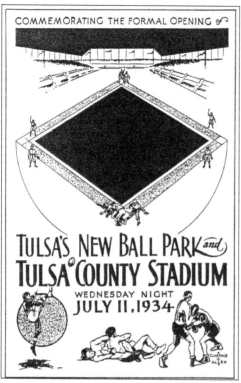

COMMEMORATING THE FORMAL OPENING of

TULSA'S NEW BALL PARK and
TULSA COUNTY STADIUM
WEDNESDAY NIGHT
JULY 11,1934

Tulsa had needed a permanent baseball stadium since McNulty Park (1919–1929) was torn down in the winter of 1930. Finally the city, county, and Oiler ownership agreed on a new location and with the help of WPA funding Tulsa County Stadium opened at Fifteenth and Sandusky on the north side of the fairgrounds. The all-wooden structure opened on July 11, 1934. It would be Tulsa's ballpark until August 30, 1980. Over the years it would be known as Texas League Park, Oiler Park, and Driller Park.

On July 11, 1997, the Tulsa Drillers honored John Stoneham, 63 years to the day that Stoneham played in the first game at Oiler Park. Ted Davis (left) was the winning pitcher in the park's final game on August 30, 1980. Davis pitched eight seasons in the minors, two with Tulsa in 1980 and 1981. He reached the AAA level with the Mets and Rangers. Both former players tossed out the ceremonial first pitch.

Top: Two notable managers for Tulsa in the 1930s were Jacob Atz (left) and Marty McManus (right). Jacob Atz is one of the all-time greats in minor league baseball history. He won seven straight pennants with Ft. Worth from 1919–1925. Atz managed over 3,500 games from 1911–1941. He was an infielder for four years in the majors from 1902–1909. Atz managed Tulsa in 1934 to the Texas League playoffs. He won 1,972 games, placing him 12th on the all-time win list. Marty McManus was an infielder with five clubs in the major leagues from 1921–1934, the last two as player-manager for the Boston Red Sox. He led the American League in doubles in 1925 and in stolen bases in 1930. He was the second baseman on Tulsa's 1920 championship team. Tulsa finished third in 1936 but won the Texas League playoffs and swept the Southern League champs, Birmingham, in the Dixie Series.

Bottom: The Texas League All-Star Game of 1938 was played in Oklahoma City. The league split into north and south division for the game with Tulsa, Oklahoma City, Ft. Worth, and Dallas in the north division. Representing Tulsa are: pitcher Max Thomas (bottom row, far left), outfielders Morris Jones (top row, far left), George Suse (top row, fourth from left) and Stan Schino (top row, eighth from left), pitcher Vern Olsen (top row, second from right), and manager Bruce Connaster (top row, far right).

27

Tony York set a Tulsa and Texas League record of reaching base safety 14 consecutive times from June 24–27, 1937. The shortstop hit seven singles, five doubles and reached base on two walks. He played 23 years (1933–1956) and over 2,700 games of minor league baseball. York played for the Chicago Cubs in 1944. His Texas League consecutive record streak was broken by Wichita's Sean McNally in 1999.

The Mad Russian Lou (his grandparents were Hungarian) Novikoff was a hard hitting, so-so leftfielder for the 1939 Oilers. He led the Texas League with a .368 batting average, pounding out 154 hits in 110 games. Novikoff started the season at Milwaukee, but after 11 games he was sent to Tulsa. After his great season with the Oilers, Novikoff was sold to Los Angeles of the Pacific Coast League. In the Angels' extended season, he had time to play 36 more games, hitting .452. Novikoff won the Minor League Player of the Year. His total numbers included 224 hits in 147 games and a .376 average. He played for the Cubs from 1941–44 and returned to the minors for six more seasons.

FOURTH INNING

Dizzy, Grayle, & Andy
Three Tulsa Legends

1940–1949

The decade of the 1940s saw major impacts in many areas. The Chicago Cubs and Cincinnati Reds made Tulsa their top farm club. Grayle Howlett became one of the Tulsa baseball's greatest owners/general managers and Dizzy Dean gave Oiler fans thrills with some of his final pitching performances.

The 1949 team won 90 games, finishing second in the regular season. They beat Ft. Worth on a dramatic three-run homer by Joe Adcock in the 11th inning of game seven in the playoffs to win the Texas League crown. Nashville took the Dixie series four games to three. 1949 was one of the more memorable years for Tulsa with all-time favorites Russ Burns, Johnny Lane, Dewey Williams, Walt Wrona, and Harry Donabedian providing the thrills. Tulsa's attendance was 33rd overall out of 448 minor league teams.

The 1949 Oilers, from left to right: (front row) Joe Adock, Johnny Lane, Harry Donabedian, Mickey Rutner, Grayle Howlett (president), Al Vincent (manager), Fletcher Robbe, Eddie Knoblauch, Russ Burns, and Dewey Williams; (back row) Lonnie Boiling (trainer), Al Boresh, Walt Wrona, Gino Marionetti, Jim Avera, Walker Cress, Frank Smith, Rube Fischer, John Bebber, Dave Jolly, and Ken Polivka.

Dutch Reuther (left), a former big league pitcher, is trying to help Dizzy Dean learn to throw sidearm. Dean, the great fireballing pitcher with the Cardinals in the 1930s, was traded to the Cubs after he injured a toe in the 1937 All-Star game. He altered his pitching motion to

compensate for the injury and that led to Dean injuring his arm. The Oilers were the Cubs' top farm team and Chicago sent Dean to Tulsa to try to throw sidearm. In his first start, a then single-game record crowd of over 7,500 fans attended the game and saw him go the distance in a 5-4 win. But the fire was gone from 'ol Diz's arm and he managed only an 8-8 record with an average of two strikeouts a game. He only pitched five more innings in the major leagues after his half-season in Tulsa.

Eddie Waitkus led the 1940 squad in 8 of 10 batting categories and played in every inning of all 162 Oiler games. The first baseman also played for the 1941 Oilers, reaching the playoff finals. Waitkus was the Chicago Cubs' first baseman from 1946–48. He was traded to the Phillies and starred on the famous 1950 Philadelphia "Whiz Kids" World Series team. Waitkus is best remembered as the inspiration for the book and movie *The Natural*. Early in his big league career, Waitkus was shot and wounded by a woman in a hotel. He recovered and went on to have an 11-year career in the major leagues.

Hank Wyse had back-to-back 20-win seasons for the 1941 and 1942 teams. His 1941 ERA of 2.09 is eighth best on the all-time Tulsa list. Wyse pitched eight years in the majors, highlighted by a 22-win season for the 1945 National League champion Chicago Cubs. Hank Wyse is the answer to a trivia question that might never change: Who threw the last pitch in a World Series game for the Chicago Cubs?

The city leaders returned baseball to Tulsa. John Mabee, P.C. Lauinger, W.K. Warren, W.L. Kistler, and William Skelly spearheaded a drive in the spring of 1945 among Tulsa's oil businessmen to revive baseball in Tulsa after World War II. Pictured is William G. Skelly, founder of Skelly Oil.

Tulsa's parent club in 1946, the Chicago Cubs, sent Grayle Howlett (right) to Tulsa to be the general manager following three dormant years during World War II. Howlett was a master promoter. Tulsa reached attendance marks that would stand until the 1990s. Under his guidance, Tulsa developed innovations such as a sleeper bus for team travel, the first regularly scheduled televised minor league games, and one of the first history and record books about minor league baseball. In the 1940s and 1950s the Mutual Radio Network broadcast a major league game of the day. Howell convinced Mutual to also air a Minor League game of the day. The first coast-to-coast broadcast of a minor league game involved Tulsa and Oklahoma City. Howlett became part owner of the Oilers in 1948. Before Howlett came to Tulsa, he worked with WGN's legendary announcer, Jack Brickhouse, on Chicago Cubs broadcasts.

Howlett (left) and park supervisor John Tabor raise the 1949 championship banner.

Howlett was known by many in the baseball business. Here Howlett talks with Baseball Commissioner Happy Chandler in 1948.

Harry Perkowski was named the Texas League Pitcher of the Year in 1948. He led the league with 22 victories. Perkowski also set the Texas League record for pinch hitting, getting 15 hits in 30 at bats. He pitched in the majors for eight years with the Reds and Cubs.

Al Vincent managed the Oilers to four successful seasons from 1948–1951. Vincent guided Tulsa to three straight Texas League Championship Series, winning it all in 1949. Nashville defeated the Oilers four games to three for the Dixie Series title. He managed Tulsa for 669 games, third on Tulsa's all-time list. Vincent won 354 games, good for fourth on the all-time win list. He managed several other minor league teams and was a coach in the majors.

Let's Goooooo Tulsa! Joe Adcock came back to Tulsa, for the first time since he was the Oilers' first baseman in 1949, when he was the manager for the 1968 Seattle Angels. The first thing he asked was "Is that guy who used to yell 'Let's Goooooo Tulsa' still here?" At the 1970 Tulsa-St. Louis exhibition game former Oiler pitcher Steve Carlton said, "You remember something about every city you play in and that yell before every Tulsa game is it. You can ask any one who played here and they'll all say the same thing." That "guy" was Andy Andrews. He started his famous yell in 1941 and soon it was an every night event at the ball park. Over the next 30 years, Andrews' yell in the bottom of the first was a booming half minute Tulsa trademark. Today, on certain nights, you can still hear Andrews' trademark call by way of recording.

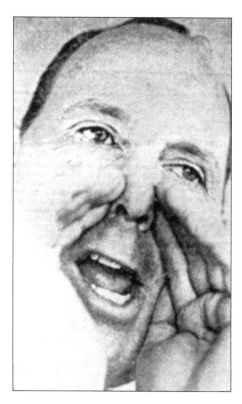

FIFTH INNING

Tough Times for Tulsa

1950–1959

The decade opened with Tulsa in a strong Texas League with cities like Ft. Worth, Dallas, Houston, San Antonio, and Oklahoma City. But the decade ended with only six teams in the league and Tulsa and San Antonio as the only major cities. Television, home air conditioning, and Dallas and Houston's try for major league expansion were the culprits. Tulsa struggled to keep major league affiliates as Cincinnati, Cleveland, Chicago Cubs, Philadelphia Phillies, and the St. Louis Cardinals all had a turn as Tulsa's parent club.

The outlook for minor league baseball in the country looked bleak as attendance and the number of teams and leagues fell to half of its peak year (1948). But owner Grayle Howlett knew that Tulsa is St. Louis Cardinal country and secured their Double A franchise for the 1959 season. And better times were on the horizon.

The 1950 season opened with the largest crowd ever to see a Tulsa baseball team in action. Dallas Eagle owner Dick Burnett had nine all-time great major league players start the Tulsa at Dallas game in Eagle uniforms. Over 53,000 saw the game played at the Cotton Bowl. The all-time greats took their positions in the top of the first inning and the Tulsa lead-off batter walked. Then the regular Dallas players took the field. The all-time greats are, from left to right, Dizzy Dean, Mickey Cochrane, Charlie Gehringer, Tris Speaker, Ty Cobb, Charlie Grimm, Duffy Lewis, Home Run Baker, and Travis Jackson. All are members of the Hall of Fame except Grimm and Lewis.

Russell "the muscle" Burns was one of the most popular players for the Oilers in the late 1940s and early '50's. Burns was a power hitting outfielder. He played for Tulsa from 1947–51, leading the league in runs batted in for two consecutive seasons in 1948–49. He set the all-time Tulsa single season RBI mark of 153 in 1949. When he was traded to rival Oklahoma City in 1952 it nearly caused a revolt among season ticket holders. Burns played minor league ball for 13 seasons, hitting 268 career home runs to go with a .298 career batting average.

Hall of Famer Rogers Hornsby was fired in the middle of the 1952 season by the St. Louis Browns. He was then hired as manager of the Cincinnati Reds. But before he took over as the Reds manager, Hornsby came to Tulsa to look over the Reds' top farm club. He spent five days with the Oilers before he took control of the Reds. Hornsby is fourth from the left in this photograph.

Joe Schultz Jr., managed the Oilers for three seasons (1952–54), winning 244 games, good for 8th on the all-time Tulsa win list. Schultz was a catcher for 11 years in the majors and 9 years in the minor leagues. He managed in the minors from 1950–1962 and was a coach for the St. Louis Cardinals from 1963–1968. He managed the Seattle Pilots in their only season in the American League. He also was interim manager with Detroit in 1973. His father was manager of Houston in the Texas League in 1931 and Joe Jr. was the bat boy. Joe Sr. allowed Joe Jr. to pinch hit in a game at age 13, making him the youngest player ever to play in a professional game. In 1952 the Fitzgerald, GA club in the Georgia State League allowed their 12 year old bat boy to play an inning—Joe Relford grounded out as a pinch hitter. Schultz (right) makes his point with the man in blue in the 1953 Texas League playoffs. (Photo courtesy Dallas Public Library, Dallas, TX.)

Johnny Vander Meer pitched back-to-back no-hitters for the Cincinnati Reds in 1938. He pitched 11 seasons for the Reds and had stops with the Cubs in 1950 and Cleveland in 1951. The Reds required Vander Meer in the spring of 1952 and sent him to Tulsa to work out the soreness in his arm. Vander Meer had one more no-hitter left in his left arm as he no-hit Beaumont 12-0 on July 15. He won 11 games for Tulsa in his last professional season.

For years the Oilers would hand out family photos of the team and their families. The 1952 Tulsa Oiler family was, from left to right: (seated) Mrs. Johnny Vander Meer with Shirley and Evelyn, Mrs. Alex Grammas, Mrs. Hobie Landrith with Carol and Gary, Mrs. Bob Curley, Mrs. LeRoy Jarvis and Jana, Mrs. Miles Jordan and Shawna, Mrs. Joe Schultz with Tommy and Mary Jo, Mrs. Leon Foulk, Mrs. Mickey Rutner with Richard and Toby, Mrs. Norman Bell and Susan, Mrs. John Temple and Michael, Mrs. Fletcher Robbe with Kathy and Michael; (second row) Trainer John Tabor, Johnny Vander Meer, Alex Grammas, Hobie Landrith, Bob Curley, LeRoy Jarvis, Niles Jordan, Manager Joe Schultz, Leon Foulk, Mickey Rutner, Norman Bell, John Temple, and Fletcher Robbe; (back row) Gail Hensley, John Walters, Leo Christante, Earl York, Frank Brown, Jack Cerin, Tommy Reis, and Jack Weisenburger.

In 1955 the Oilers were an affiliate of Cleveland. The Indians sent a young Roger Maras to Tulsa. Maras played outfield 25 games for Tulsa and hit one home run as an Oiler, just 60 short of the major league record he would set six years later with the Yankees. To help the media and fans pronounce his name correctly, Maras had his name legally changed to Maris while playing in Tulsa.

CHUCK HARMON
third base CINCIN. REDLEGS

Charles Harmon was the first African American to play for Tulsa. Harmon, a third baseman, led the 1953 Oilers in hits, total bases, stolen bases, and batting average. He also had an 18-game hitting streak. Harmon played in the majors from 1954–1957 with Cincinnati, Philadelphia, and St. Louis. (Photo of 1954 Topps baseball card.)

Hall of Famer Frank Robinson played eight games at second and third base for Tulsa during the 1954 season, hitting .267 before being sent down to Single A. But Robinson never played a game in Tulsa. The Oilers started the season on the road, and were rained out of their first series at home before going back on the road. Robinson went to Columbia, SC, before Tulsa returned home. (Photo Courtesy of the National Baseball Hall of Fame Library, Cooperstown, NY.)

For almost 30 years, the Tulsa Diamond Dinner was one of the top " hot-stove league" events in baseball, major or minor leagues. Current stars and former big league greats by the dozens made it a terrific event. Here Mickey Mantle receives the Oklahoma Outstanding Major League Player Award for the 1955 season.

KRMG

Mack Creager

Hugh Finnerty

Tulsa has been fortunate to have great radio play-by-play announcers throughout the years. Mack Creager (left) broadcast for the Oilers from 1948–1971 and Drillers in 1977, announcing over 3,000 games on radio and TV. Hugh Finnerty (right) was the team public relations director in the early 1950s and general manager in the early 1960s. He broadcast over 1,200 games in those two decades. Finnerty won the 1963 *Sporting News* Minor League Executive of the Year Award and the 1965 National Association of Minor League Baseball Award for Attendance. That season, Tulsa was fourth in the country out of 106 minor league teams. He was also President of the Texas League from 1965–'69.

Each year owner Grayle Howlett would patch and paint up old wooden Texas League Park for another season. Howlett had a special paint job for Oklahoma's semi-centennial in 1957.

Player-manager Al Widmar was one of the most popular managers in the 1950s. Widmar had pitched in the majors for five seasons (1947–1952). He played for Tulsa from 1955–58. Widmar led the team in ERA in 1955 and wins in 1955 and 1956. He became a player-manager in 1956–58, guiding the Oilers to the playoffs in 1956 and 1957. In his three seasons as manager, Widmar pitched Tulsa to 22 wins. He went on to be a pitching coach in the major leagues for over 20 years.

John "Pepper" Martin had an outstanding career as a third baseman and outfielder for the St. Louis Cardinals from 1928–1944. He lived in the Tulsa area after his playing days. The Oilers hired him as a coach in 1957. He coached for Tulsa through the 1963 season. He took to the broadcast booth during games, cutting a hole in the screen in the radio booth so he could hang a fish net out of the booth to try to catch foul balls, 20 years before Harry Caray did it on national cable TV. He was the oldest player to play professional baseball—during the 1958 season when he pinch-ran for Tulsa in a game at age 54.

SIXTH INNING

The Golden Decade

1960–1969

The affiliate switch to the St. Louis Cardinals in 1959 helped on the field, but attendance dropped below the break even mark. Declining attendance was a problem all across minor league baseball. Grayle Howlett was hours from moving the team to Albuquerque, but Tulsa businessman A. Ray Smith came to the rescue as part owner and the Oilers stayed in Tulsa. The Oilers made the playoffs eight times in the decade with exciting Cardinal farm hands. Attendance rose to near record levels. Smith, who bought out Howlett in 1961, moved Tulsa into Triple A in 1966. The highlight of the decade was the 1968 Oilers. They won more games (99) than any other Triple A team in the decade. Tulsa won the Eastern Division of the Pacific Coast League by 18 games and blasted Spokane four games to one for the championship. The 1968 Tulsa Oilers were one of the most dominant teams in the history of minor league baseball.

The 1968 Oilers, from left to right: (front row) Kenny Moore (clubhouse attendant), Coco Laboy, Elio Chacon, Clay Kirby, Warren Spahn (manager), Jim Hutto, Steve Huntz, Pete Mikkelsen, and Bill Elias (batboy); (middle row) Jack Boag-trainer, Floyd Wicker, Chuck Taylor, Jim Hicks, Mike Torrez, Dick LeMay, Ramon Hernandez, Pedro Gonzalez, and Titus Robertson (park superintendent); (back row) Dave Pavlesic, Danny Breeden, Jerry Robertson, Joe Hague, Tom Hilgendorf, Sal Campisi, Bob Sadowski, and Gary Geiger.

Tulsa won the Texas League playoffs in 1960 and faced the Mexico City Tigers in the Pan American Series. This replaced the tie-in with the Southern League and the Dixie Series. The Oilers defeated Mexico City four games to one to become the champions. Co-owners Grayle Howlett (left) and A. Ray Smith display the 1960 championship banner.

The St. Louis Cardinals, now the parent club of the Oilers, began a 12 year series of exhibition games in Tulsa. On July 28, 1960, the Redbirds made their first visit to Tulsa since 1946. The largest attendance in the 47 year history of Texas League/Oiler Park (10,023) saw the Cards defeat Tulsa 12–5. Hall of Fame outfielder Stan Musial (left) and Hall of Fame broadcaster Harry Caray pause for a photo before the game.

Two of the most popular players to ever wear a Tulsa uniform were Joe Patterson and Jim Beauchamp. Patterson was a lighting quick outfielder for five seasons (1962–65 and 1967). He led the league in steals for three consecutive seasons (1962–64) and in runs scored in 1964. Nicknamed "Speedo" by radio announcer Len Morton, Patterson would bring the fans to their feet with his base stealing and excellent outfield play.

Jim Beauchamp played for the Oilers six seasons (1959–1961, 1963–64, and 1974). The hard-hitting outfielder is best remembered for his outstanding 1963 season when he led the team to the playoff championship. His .337 average was second in the league and he led the Oilers in every offensive category except stolen bases (he was second!). He hit 31 home runs, the most by an Oiler since Guy Sturdy hit 49 in 1926. It was the most homers hit by a Tulsan in the history of Texas League/Oiler/Driller Park (1934-1980). Beauchamp played for five major league clubs from 1964-1973. He came back to Tulsa as a player-coach and hit a home run in the 15th inning of the sixth game of the 1974 American Association championship to help the Oilers win. He was a coach for the Atlanta Braves during their great winning seasons of 1991–1998.

Oiler Park was built as a WPA project in 1933–34. Originally called Texas League Park, it was renamed Oiler Park in 1962 by owner A. Ray Smith. The old all-wooden structure was past its prime and as early as 1956, management tried to get new facilities, but nothing was done. Each year Smith would repair and paint as much as the old ballpark could handle. Oiler Park was a perfect place to watch a game. You were right on top of the players, the broadcast and newspaper booths were set right on top of the action. And park supervisor John Tabor had one of the best groomed fields in all of minor league baseball.

TEXAS LEAGUE PARK

4400 EAST 15TH

Friday Nite, April 27th

GAME TIME 8:00 P. M.

Those Nationally Famous

Negro American League

INDIANAPOLIS

CLOWNS

VS. THE CRACK

Buster HAYWOOD
PLAYING MANAGER
of Negro American League
CLOWNS

KANSAS CITY
MONARCHS

Half of Park for Colored Patrons

Through the years, over 100 major league exhibition games have been played in Tulsa, including dozens of Negro League games. Here is a newspaper ad promoting a 1951 game. Negro League games were played through 1962 in Tulsa.

The Diamond Dinner under A. Ray Smith's direction provided dozens of great baseball stars. Pictured from the 1963 dinner are, from left to right, Andy Andrews (Oiler front office), Ralph Terry (New York Yankees), A. Ray Smith, Pepper Martin (Oiler coach), and a hungry Joe Garagiola.

Speaking to the crowd from the 1961 Diamond Dinner is Hall of Famer Branch Rickey. Rickey played and managed in the majors from 1905–1925. He was the general manager for the Cardinals, Dodgers, and Pirates. He is credited with inventing the farm system.

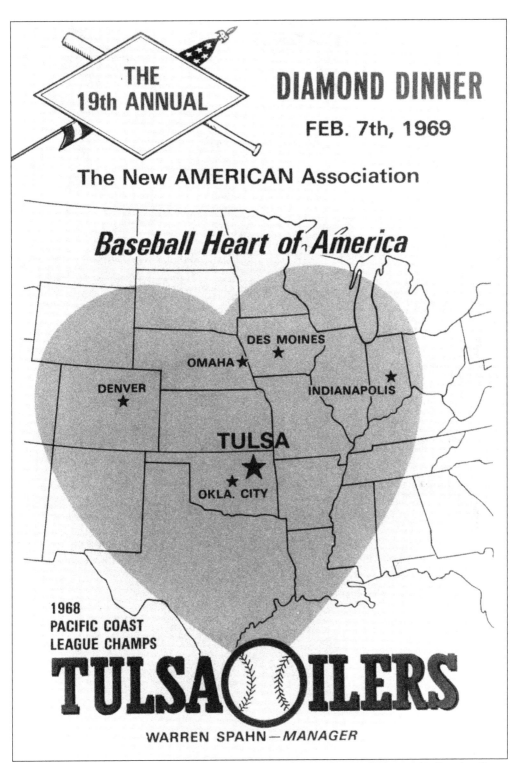

Each Diamond Dinner had a theme. The 1969 dinner honored the 1968 Pacific Coast League Champions.

On May 5, 1966, Tulsa hosted the St. Louis Cardinals for an exhibition game at the University of Tulsa's football field, Skelly Stadium. It was Tulsa's first year of Triple A and Oiler owner A. Ray Smith spent $16,500 for rent and baseball improvements to the field. A large backstop was set-up in the west corner of the north end zone.

Because of the short right field foul line of 208 feet a screen was set up in right field. 18,904 fans saw the Cardinals beat Tulsa 5–4. The attendance is still the record for a baseball game in the state of Oklahoma.

Steve Carlton pitched for Tulsa in four games in 1964, and then was 9-5 in 1966, leading the playoff team in ERA. "Lefty" went on to have a 24-year career in the major leagues, winning 329 games, 9th on the all-time win chart. He was second in career strikeouts with 4,136. Carlton was elected to the Baseball Hall of Fame in 1994.

Warren Spahn was named Oiler manager in 1967. He guided the Oilers from 1967–1971 through 711 games, the second most games for a Tulsa manager in history. His teams won 372 games, good for third place on the all-time list. In 1967 Spahn pitched for Tulsa in three games, starting two. He guided the Oilers to the 1968 Pacific Coast League Championship. The '68 squad is considered one of the best in minor league history. Spahn pitched 20 years in the major leagues, primarily with the Braves, winning 363 games, a record for left-handers and fifth best in major league history. He was elected to the Baseball Hall of Fame in 1973. He earned the prestigious Purple Heart and Bronze Star in World War II.

Charlie Metro managed the Oilers their first year in Triple A, in 1966. Tulsa was in a heated pennant race with Indianapolis the entire season. Late in August, Tulsa took a two-game lead when both teams went into losing streaks. Tulsa lost eight in a row and Indianapolis six.

Sports Section   # TULSA WORLD   *Sports Section*

TULSA, OKLAHOMA, SUNDAY, AUGUST 21, 1966

OILERS LOSE 9TH STRAIGHT, PAD LEAD

On August 20, Tulsa was tied with Indianapolis when the Oilers and lost their ninth straight, but the Indians dropped a doubleheader to give Tulsa a half-game lead. The next day, the headline in the Tulsa World was one of the most remembered in Tulsa sports history, "Tulsa loses 9th in a row, Pad lead." The Oilers went on to win the Eastern Division but fell to Seattle four game to three in the championship series.

57

The Oilers had dozens of great players during the 1960s. Sal Campisi won 25 games and lost only 5 for Tulsa in 1968 and 1969. He won the American Association Pitcher of the Year Award with a microscopic 1.99 ERA.

Coco Laboy was a hard hitting infielder who batted .308 in '66, .298 in '67, and .292 in 1968, when he also led the league with 100 RBIs.

Larry Jaster pitched for Tulsa for parts of three seasons, winning 19 games. Jaster is best remembered for pitching a post-season playoff game that decided who won the 1965 Texas League Eastern crown. Jaster pitched a complete 2-0 victory over Dallas-Ft. Worth.

Roy Majtyka was an infielder on the 1963–64 playoff teams. He became a standout manager in the minors for 26 seasons, winning 1,832 games. Majtyka ranks 18th in all-time wins as a minor league manager.

Dal Maxvill was hitting .348 for the Oilers when he was called up to the Cardinals in 1962. He played 14 years in the majors and was the St. Louis Cardinals general manager from 1985–1994.

Mike Shannon was an outfielder on the 1961 playoff team. He was a crowd favorite for his roles in the annual "Oiler Frolics" night. Players would try their best on musical instruments and take part in variety acts in pre-game ceremonies.

Chuck Taylor played for Tulsa for parts of four seasons and won 38 games. He is the last Tulsa pitcher to win 20 games in a season. He won 18 in the regular season in 1968 and two in the post-season, including a complete game 1-0 shutout in the championship game. He pitched eight seasons in the major leagues.

Walt "No Neck" Williams was a hustling outfielder who hit .330 for the 1965 playoff team and .330 for the 1966 playoff team. He came back to Tulsa after a 10-year big league career to be the hitting coach for the Drillers in 1989 and 1990.

Tulsa businessman A. Ray Smith became co-owner of the Tulsa Oilers in 1961, and in 1962 he bought owner Grayle Howlett's interest and kept the team from moving. Under Smith's leadership the city caught baseball fever and attendance rose as high as third and fourth in the country for a minor league team. He helped Tulsa become a Triple A city in 1966. After years of battles with city and county officials on stadium improvements, Smith moved the franchise to New Orleans in 1977. Smith continued operating the franchise in Louisville where all-time minor league attendance records were recorded.

Ted Simmons won the American Association Rookie of the Year Award in 1969. The switch-hitting catcher hit .317 with 158 hits in 129 games. He played 21 seasons in the major leagues, and later became the general manager of the Pittsburgh Pirates.

SEVENTH INNING

From Boom to Bust

1970–1979

The early 1970s saw Tulsa in Triple A baseball, with good attendance (8th in the nation in 1971, 6th in 1972), and with the parent club, the St. Louis Cardinals, sending exciting players to Tulsa, helping them win back-to-back championships. The end of the decade saw Tulsa in Double A in a make shift ballpark. The players said the moon had a smoother surface than the Driller Park infield, and attendance fell to 700 a game.

The Tulsa Oilers won back-to-back American Association Championships in 1973 and 1974. Pictured here are the 1973 champions, from left to right: (front row) Jim Dwyer, Buzz Nitschke, Tim Plodinec, Greg Terlecky, Marc Hill, Ray Bare, Jack Krol-manager, Mike Thompson, Tommy Thompson, Bob Forsch and Ike Brookens; (back row) Titus Robertson (park superintendent), Tom Heintzelman, Bill Stein, Doug Clark, Mike Nagy, Danny Godby, Don Durham, Byron Browne, Johnny B. Wockenfuss, Dan McGinn, Alan Putz, Keith Hernandez, Stan Papi, Larry Milbourne, Gene Dusan, and Jack Boag (trainer).

The annual Cardinal exhibition game against the Oilers drew near-capacity crowds. The stands are packed for the May 17, 1971 game. The Oilers won this one 9-2.

The front office is critical to any minor league team. Tulsa has had great office personnel in its history. Tulsa's attendance was eighth in the country in 1971 and sixth in 1972. The Oiler office staff is pictured here. Jim Weigel (bottom) went on to be a minor league general manager for many years. Forrest Cameron (top left) was public relations director and radio announcer. He later founded the *Greater Tulsa Reporter* newspapers. Len Morton (top right) was the voice of Oiler baseball from 1962–1973. Morton became a top cable television sales executive in Tulsa. Morton was known for his trademark at the end of each home victory by the Oilers. Shortly after the game, Morton asked the crowd leaving Oiler Park to honk their cars in appreciation for the team's winning efforts. Immediately after the request you could hear horns blare away behind him during the wrap-up show.

Legendary Negro League pitcher Leroy "Satchel" Paige was a front office employee/coach for Tulsa from 1973–1976. He spoke to civic clubs and kids baseball leagues around Tulsa. For 22 years Paige pitched in the Negro Leagues. Then on his 42nd birthday, in 1948, Cleveland Indians owner Bill Veeck brought Paige to the major leagues. He continued to play either major league or Triple A baseball consistently until 1959. He was named to the Baseball Hall of Fame in 1971.

In 1973, Jim Dwyer had the second highest batting average in Tulsa history, hitting .387 and winning the American Association batting title. Presenting the trophy to Dwyer are league president Joe Ryan and Joe Medwick, the Cardinal's minor league hitting instructor.

Tulsa outfielder Danny Godby was presented an outboard boat motor as the most popular Oiler of 1974 when he hit .344. Presenting the prize are, from left to right, Hall of Famer Joe Medwick, Godby, Oiler coach Satchel Paige, and Bob Kennedy, the St. Louis Cardinal farm director.

In 1975 and 1976, Paul "Daffy" Dean was director of the Tulsa Oiler baseball instructional camp for kids. The brother of Dizzy Dean, he pitched for the Cardinals from 1934–1939, the Giants from 1940–41, and the Browns in 1943. He won 19 consecutive games over two seasons in 1934–35.

Ken Boyer, a former MVP third baseman for the Cardinals, was the Tulsa manager for three successful seasons from 1974–76. He guided the Oilers to the 1974 American Association championship. His 218 victories place him in 10th place on the all-time win list.

The following pages show several outstanding players for the Oilers in the first half of the decade. Hector Cruz won the *Sporting News* Minor League Player of the Year Award in 1975. Cruz hit 29 home runs and had 116 RBIs, both league highs. He had a seven-year big league career, and is the brother of major leaguer and former Oiler, Jose Cruz.

John Denny won 9 games for the 1974 championship team. He won the 1983 National League Cy Young Award for the pennant winning Phillies, and played 13 years in the majors.

Bob Forsch won 20 games for the 1973–74 championship clubs. He tossed a nine inning no-hitter for Tulsa in 1973. He pitched 16 years in the big leagues, 15 of them with the Cardinals.

Mick Kelleher was one of the greatest defensive shortstops in Tulsa history. He led the American Association in fielding in 1972 with a .979 average and again in 1975 with a .978 average, the highest marks in Tulsa history. He was part of the 1972 team that set a record 62 games in a season without an error and fewest errors by a team in a season—114 in 136 games. He played 11 years in the major leagues.

Marc Hill was called up from Double A with 10 games to go in the 1973 season and Tulsa in a tight pennant race. Hill hit .414 for the Oilers and along with Keith Hernandez was a leader of the "Cardiac Kids." They were so-named by Tulsa Tribune sports writer Dick Suagee for their knack of winning games in the late innings. A catcher, Hill hit .278 for Tulsa in 1974, winning the league Rookie of the Year award, as Tulsa won consecutive titles. He played in the big leagues for 14 seasons.

Keith Hernandez came up with a month to go in 1973 and hit .333 to help Tulsa win the crown. In 1974 he hit .351 and won the batting title. Late in the year he was called up to the Cardinals. Over parts of four seasons with the Oilers, Hernandez played in 229 games getting 278 hits. He won the National League co-MVP in 1979 with the Cardinals. Hernandez played for 17 seasons in the major leagues.

Bake McBride played outfield for Tulsa in 1972 and 1973. He was the National League Rookie of the Year in 1974 with the Cardinals, and played 11 seasons in the majors. His real first name is Arnold.

Ken Reitz was an excellent defensive third baseman for the 1972 club that set the Tulsa all-time record for fielding. He was named as the post season American Association all-star third baseman. Reitz led the team in RBIs, and became the first man to play for both the Tulsa Oilers and Tulsa Drillers. He played third base 45 games for the Drillers in 1985, and went on to have an 11-year career with five major league teams. He won a Gold Glove in 1975 and started the 1980 All-Star Game.

Garry Templeton was a flashy shortstop in 1976, hitting .321. He led the team in stolen bases, triples, and hits. Templeton played 16 years in the major leagues. He became the first switch-hitter to have 100 hits from both sides of the plate in the same season—1979, when he was with the Cardinals. He retired following the 1991 season. He was the last Tulsa Oiler to play in the major leagues.

Bob Carpenter started his outstanding sports broadcasting career in 1976 with the Oilers as a radio announcer. He has been the TV voice of several major league teams including the Twins, Cardinals, Rangers, and Mets. Since 1988 Carpenter has been an ESPN announcer, primarily covering major league baseball and college basketball.

Jerry Mumphrey was a speedy outfielder in 1975 and 1976. He was hitting .338 when he was called up in May of 1976. In 1975, he led Tulsa in stolen bases, base hits, triples and runs scored. Mumphrey played for five teams in a 15-year big league career.

When Oiler owner A. Ray Smith took the Oilers to New Orleans in October of 1976 it looked like there would be no more baseball in Tulsa. In January 1977, however, building contractor Bill Rollings obtained the Texas Rangers Double A franchise from Lafayette, Louisiana, and Tulsa re-entered the Texas League. In a fan contest, Drillers was selected as a nickname. The team would play in Oiler Park, but it was renamed Driller Park. Tragedy struck at an exhibition game played April 3, 1977 between Houston and Texas. Over 5,000 fans crammed the old ball park. A sudden shower came up and too many fans in a small section under the right field roof caused structural failure. Seventeen people fell 20 feet to the concrete walkway below as a 15-foot section collapsed. The Drillers played in what remained of the stadium for four bleak seasons. Country music entertainer Roy Clark was the team co-owner with Rollings for six years.

One of the Drillers' top pitchers was their first—Danny Darwin. Darwin won 13 games and lost 4 for the Drillers in 1977. He led the playoff team in wins, strikeouts, and ERA. Darwin was also a Texas League All-Star. He pitched for 21 seasons in the major leagues, from 1978–1998. Darwin led the National League with a 2.21 ERA in 1990.

The first manager of Tulsa under the Driller nickname was former big league infielder Marty Martinez. He played for six teams in seven seasons. Martinez guided the Drillers to the first half-title in 1977. In the final game of the 1977 season he pitched a complete game allowing nine hits and four earned runs. He later coached for several seasons in the major leagues and was interim manager of the Seattle Mariners in 1986.

Eddie Miller holds the all-time single season stolen base record for Tulsa with 80 in 1977. He played in just 100 games for the Drillers. The outfielder on the '77 playoff team had 110 hits and was a member of the Texas League All-Star team. He played parts of seven seasons in the majors with four teams.

Although Dave Righetti only pitched in 13 games for Tulsa in 1978, he is remembered for setting a Texas League record. On July 16, 1978 Righetti set the all-time Tulsa and Texas League record for strikeouts in a single game—21. He left the game after 9 innings with the score tied at 2-2. Tulsa eventually lost to Midland 4-2 in 10 innings. He pitched 91 innings for the Drillers, striking out 127 batters. In Righetti's 16-year major league career he won the American League Rookie of the Year award in 1981 with the Yankees, pitched a no-hitter on July 4, 1983, and won 33 games in three years as a starter. He saved 252 games in 13 seasons as a relief pitcher. Righetti later became a successful pitching coach for the San Francisco Giants.

Billy Sample was a Texas League All-Star outfielder on the 1977 playoff team. He led the team in average (.348), runs, hits, doubles, triples, and RBIs. He also hit for the cycle. He played nine seasons in majors with a .272 career batting average. Sample later was a radio and television announcer with TBS and ESPN. He is now an analyst with mlb.com.

Marty Scott was a versatile player for the Drillers in 1977–78 and 1981, and he managed the team in 1983. In 1978 he hit .318 and played first base, third base, and outfielder. He led the team in runs, hits, doubles, RBIs and batting average, and was named to Texas League All-Star team. He played all nine positions in the 1981 All-Star game! Scott was the Texas Rangers minor league farm director in the late '80s and early '90s. He was the manager of the St. Paul Saints of the independent Northern League in the late '90s and is now directing the Ft. Worth club in the independent Central League.

No, this is not a photograph of an early morning workout. This was taken at a game at Driller Park in 1979. The team play and the facilities were not even remotely attractive. The average attendance fell to only 700 a game. On June 26th a 3.7 million dollar bond issue for a new baseball stadium on the fairgrounds failed by 2,000 votes. It looked like 1979 would be the last year of professional baseball in Tulsa.

EIGHTH INNING

From Bust to Boom

1980–1989

For Tulsa baseball, the 1980s were the opposite of the 1970s. The decade began with Tulsa drawing only 850 fans a game in a dilapidated stadium. But by the end of the '80s a new stadium, a general manager with enthusiasm, and a new hands-on owner took Tulsa once again to new baseball heights.

The 1982 Drillers in the first half of the season were bad—very bad. In the second half, the Drillers were good—very good. After playing 19 games under .500 in the first half, Tulsa turned it around on the strength of pitching and timely hitting, playing 23 games above .500, winning the second half championship and sweeping El Paso for the Texas League title.

The 1982 champion Drillers, from left to right: (seated) Chuck Lamson (operations director), Kevin Richards, Daryl Smith, Cha Cho Gonzalez, Tom Henke, Jim Gideon, Dennis Long, and Al Lachowicz; (second row) Joe Nemeth-trainer, Jim Maxwell, Dan Murphy, Shake Moore, Tommy Dunbar, Brad Mengwasser, Marty Leach, Mike Mason, Dave Stockstill, Bobby Ball, and George Willis (assistant general manager); (third row) Hal O'Halloran (radio announcer), Dave Moharter (coach), Tim Henry, Donnie Scott, Carmelo Aguayo, Oscar Meija, Jerry Neufang, Ron Gooch, Mike Jirschele, Tommy Burgess (manager), and Merrill Eckstein (general manager). Eckstein came to Tulsa in 1980 and oversaw the building of new Sutton Stadium that tripled attendance from the last season in old Driller Park. Through his efforts the 1981 and 1982 Texas League All-Star Game was played at Sutton Stadium.

Sutton Stadium, still under construction on December 12, 1980. Tulsa Drillers owner Bill Rollings, city, and county officials agreed on a new stadium when Tulsa oilman Robert Sutton donated most of the money. On April 16, 1981 the 4,800-seat stadium opened. When Sutton Stadium opened it had an artificial surface and was also used for high school football and soccer.

Robert Sutton—would we have a great baseball stadium today without him?.

Sutton Stadium, April 1981.

Pete O'Brien was the first baseman for the 1981 Drillers. He led the playoff team in home runs and RBIs. O'Brien drove in the first two Driller runs in the history of the stadium. He hit the first homer in the stadium's history on April 17, 1981. He also hit the third that night. O'Brien played 12 seasons in the major leagues with four teams.

Tom Burgess managed Tulsa to two consecutive playoff berths in 1981 and 1982, winning the title in 1982. Burgess was also a coach on the 1968 PCL Champion Oilers club. He played two seasons in the major leagues.

Mike Jirschele played third base and shortstop a Driller record 405 games for Tulsa in 1980–82, '85, and '87. He became a successful minor league manager in the Kansas City Royal organization, winning the *Sporting News* Minor League Manager.of the Year Award in 1994.

Ronnie Darling of Yale University was the first choice in the summer 1981 draft. He was chosen by the Texas Rangers and assigned to Tulsa. Due to the major league players' strike of '81, Darling's first two starts for the Drillers created a great deal of national media attention. He won 4 games in 13 starts for the Drillers. Darling won 136 major league games in 13 seasons.

Tommy Dunbar was the batting leader on the '82 champion Drillers, hitting .323. He led the club in seven batting categories. Dunbar played three seasons for the Texas Rangers.

Tom Henke pitched for the Driller playoff teams in 1981–82. He led the '82 championship team in saves and finished 42 games. Henke had a 14-year big league career with 311 lifetime saves.

Two of the most versatile players for the Drillers were Steve Buechele and Tracy Cowger. Buechele played second and third base and hit .296 for the '82 champs and .277 in 1983. He played infield for 11 seasons in the major leagues.

The versatile Tracy Cowger played catcher, third base, designated hitter, and outfield for Tulsa for four seasons (1980–83). He had 267 hits in 290 games for the Drillers.

Kevin Buckley was a first baseman for Tulsa in 1983. He was in a home run duel all season with teammate Mike Rubel. Rubel had 23 home runs when he was called up to Triple A in early August. Buckley hit his 31st and 32nd home runs of the season in his final two at-bats in the last game of the year. It was the most home runs for a Tulsa player in a season since 1927. Buckley played five games in the major leagues for the Rangers in 1984.

Joe Preseren was hired as the Tulsa Drillers general manager in September, 1983. In his 12 seasons as Driller GM, Preseren increased attendance a record 11 straight seasons and set a then all-time attendance mark in 1994 with 344,764 fans. Many of those seasons had a poor to mediocre won-loss record on the field. He oversaw several stadium expansions and improvements. In 1987 and 1993 Preseren won the Texas League Executive of the Year award. He was honored by the Sporting News as Double A executive of the year in 1987 and 1990. The Oklahoma Jaycees named him as a State of Oklahoma Outstanding Young Oklahoman in 1995. His love of the game of baseball and the fan friendly atmosphere he helped create made Drillers Stadium the summer place to be. Today, Joe and his family live in Roanoke, Virginia with their three daughters and son.

In 1983 Sutton Stadium's name was changed to Tulsa County Stadium. Robert Sutton, who donated most of the funds to build the stadium, was allegedly involved in an illegal oil pricing scheme. In 1984 the seating capacity was increased to 7,500.

Ruben Sierra played outfield for Tulsa in 1985 leading the Drillers in RBIs, runs, hits, doubles, triples, and stolen bases. Here he pulls into third base with one of his league-leading triples. Manager Orlando Gomez, the Driller manager, is at left. Sierra made the major leagues in 1986. Over the next 17 season with five teams, Sierra played in over 1,700 games with over 1,800 hits, appearing in four All-Star games. He was on the Texas Rangers' active roster at the start of spring training 2003.

Kenny Rogers (left) and Kevin Brown (opposite) both played for the Drillers in parts of the 1986–88 seasons. Rogers won only five games in 59 starts. But in 178 innings he struck out 151. Rogers has played 14 seasons winning over 150 games in the major leagues, and is on the active list as the 2003 season opens. He pitched a perfect game for Texas in 1994.

Kevin Brown won 14 games for Tulsa, including 12 in the 1988 Texas League championship year. Brown has pitched 16 years in the majors for five teams winning over 180 games. He was named to the All-Star team five times. Brown was with the Dodgers as the 2003 season opened.

Steve Wilson had a tremendous 1988 season for Tulsa, winning 15 games in the regular season and 3 more in the playoffs. Wilson played six seasons in the major leagues.

Jim Skaalen managed Tulsa one year, but what a productive season. Attendance was the best in 16 years. After finishing second in the first half, the Drillers won the second half by a half game. Tulsa swept Shreveport in the first round and defeated El Paso in the finals, four games to two. Skaalen was named 1988 Texas League manager of the year.

On July 18, 1988, Tulsa hosted an exhibition game with the USA Olympic team and the South Korean team. One-handed hurler Jim Abbott fanned eight in six innings for the win. Future big league stars Robin Ventura, Andy Benes, Ben McDonald, Charles Nagy, and Tino Martinez were on the USA team that won 7-3.

On opening night 1989 an overflow crowd of 13,988 saw Tulsa win 10-6 over Shreveport. It was the largest crowd to date in Tulsa baseball history and helped spur stadium expansion plans in the 1990s.

Two of the power leaders of 1989 were Gary Alexander (left) and Dean Palmer. Alexander, a first baseman for Tulsa from 1988–90, had 32 home runs and 143 RBIs in his career. He hit the game-winning home run in the final game of the 1988 championship series. Palmer pounded out a league-leading 25 home runs and drove in 90 runs in 1989. The third baseman played 13 seasons in the major leagues, hitting over 270 home runs. He was on the Detroit roster as the 2003 season began.

Juan Gonzalez hit 21 home runs and had 85 RBIs for the 1989 Drillers. Gonzalez has had a fabulous career, hitting over 400 home runs in 14 seasons. He won the American League Most Valuable Player award in 1996 and 1998, and was still playing for the Texas Rangers as the 2003 season opened.

Sammy Sosa was a crowd favorite even with the Tulsa Drillers in 1989. On opening night he hit an inside-the-park home run at Drillers Stadium. Sosa hit seven homers and hit .297 in 66 games before he was sent to Triple A for 10 games. Later that year he was traded to the White Sox. Sosa and Mark McGwire set the baseball world on its ear with their great home run race of 1998. As the 2003 season opened, Sosa had 499 career home runs in his 14-year big league career.

The Texas Rangers played four exhibition games in Tulsa during the decade. In 1989 creative autograph hounds found a way to get the players' attention.

Although all-time strikeout king Nolan Ryan did not play in the 1989 game, he did sign dozens of autographs.

Opposite: The 1998 Tulsa Drillers, from left to right: (front row) John Powell, Warren Morris, Andy Barkett, Bruce Crabbe (coach), Bobby Jones (manager), Brad Arnsberg (coach), Mike Venafro, Brandon Knight, and Doug O'Neill; (middle row) Chad Mottola, Ramsey Koeyers, Chris Michalak, Scott Watkins, Jason Goligoski, Cesar King, Chris Demetral, Jason Conti, Cliff Brumbaugh, and Mike Quinn (trainer); (back row) Scott Podsednik, Dave Tuttle, Rob Sasser, Dan Smith, Dan Kolb, Andrew Vessel, David Manning, Ryan Glynn, and Sean Collins.

Ninth Inning

Record Setting Times
and Disappointments

1990–2002

Tulsa's baseball fortunes continued into the 1990s. Attendance continued to soar, Drillers Stadium continued to be expanded and improved, and many individual records were set. But in this period there were two major disappointments. In 1991 Tulsa was one of a dozen cities in line for a Triple A franchise. Tulsa was in the field that was narrowed down to five; Charlotte, North Carolina, and Ottawa, Canada, were finally selected. No problem with Charlotte, a city with years of rich baseball history. A dozen years later that franchise is flourishing. The other was a great mistake. Ottawa had not had professional baseball for 30 years and was within an hours drive from major league baseball. Its nearest opponent is four hours driving time. Tulsa's is an hour and a half from Oklahoma City. The last six seasons, Tulsa has outdrawn Ottawa by over a hundred thousand fans a year. After Ottawa and Charlotte were admitted to the International League, the chairman of the Triple A expansion committee was named president of the International League.

Hmmmmm.

Tulsa's 26 year major league affiliate, the Texas Rangers, were sold and the new owner decided he wanted to own his Double A team, so the Drillers were left looking for a new major league affiliate. Still, Tulsa won the 1998 Texas League title in record setting fashion. In the first half the Drillers were in last place, 14 games out. But with a talent upgrade and manager Bobby Jones' guidance, Tulsa roared to almost a .700 pace to win the second half. Arkansas fell in the Eastern Division finals and Tulsa won the championship in a thrilling seven-game series.

The 1990 Texas League All-Star Game was played at Drillers Stadium. Three Driller players named to the squad were, from left to right, outfielder Kevin Belcher, first baseman Rob Maurer, and catcher Bill Haselman. Shreveport's Bill Evers was the East manager. Tulsa also hosted the 1999 Texas League All-Star game. A crowd of 9,374 was the largest attendance for the event in the United States since 1966. The Texas League also played a few All-Star games against the Mexican League in Mexico City.

Ivan Rodriguez was an outstanding catcher for Tulsa in the first two and half months of the 1991 season. It was a rare sight when an opposing runner tried to steal. He threw out runners at a 60% rate. In June, the Drillers had advertised for several days that Rodriguez and his fiancée, Maribel, were to be married June 20 between games of a double header at home plate. The Texas Rangers called Rodriquez up the day before the ceremony. The couple was married two days later. Rodriquez played 12 seasons for Texas winning 10 Gold Glove awards. He was named to the American League All-Star team 10 consecutive seasons from 1992–2001. He started the 2003 season with the Florida Marlins.

Walt Wrona was a catcher on three consecutive playoff teams, from 1948–50. His best season was the '49 Dixie Series' team when he hit .344. He played for Tulsa in 1951 and Oklahoma City in 1952. After finishing his playing career he settled his family in Tulsa. All three of his sons played professional baseball.

Rick Wrona was a catcher for Tulsa in 1991. This made the Wrona's the first father-son combo to play for Tulsa. Rick had a 14-year professional career. He played seven seasons in the majors. In 1990 he was with Iowa, the Cubs Triple A team, with his brother Bill Wrona, who also played eight years of professional baseball. Another brother, Ron Wrona, played pro ball for seven seasons.

Rusty Greer played three seasons as a Driller from 1991–93 as a first baseman and outfielder, getting 253 hits in 255 games. He returned to the Drillers three times on medical rehab in 2000, 2001 and 2002, playing a total of nine games. The 2003 season will be Greer's 10th with Texas.

Went Hubbard purchased the Tulsa Drillers in November, 1986. Hubbard has been a hands-on owner. You might see the distinguished looking white haired Hubbard cleaning the relish and mustard stand, or taking tickets or in the stands talking to fans about prices or starting times. He has upgraded Drillers Stadium to its present capacity of 11,003—the largest Double A stadium—and kept the Drillers as one of the top teams in the minor leagues today, both financially and at the gate. In 1999 the Tulsa Drillers won the John H. Johnson President's trophy that annually honors minor league baseball's best all-around franchise. After Hubbard received the award at the December, 1999 baseball winter meetings Hubbard said, "We should not forget the fans of the Tulsa Drillers are who made this all possible." The Drillers also were named the Double A franchise of the year in 1992 by Baseball America magazine. Hubbard's son Jeff was a Tulsa Driller coach in 1991.

In 1993, The Drillers honored the 25th anniversary of Tulsa's 1968 Pacific Coast League champions. Former owner A. Ray Smith (left) visits with Hubbard.

Before he was elected governor of the state of Texas, George W. Bush was an owner of the Texas Rangers from 1989–1994. On April 11, 1991, Texas played Tulsa in an exhibition game at Driller Stadium. Hubbard and Bush toured Drillers Stadium before the game. (Photo by Darryl Wilson, *Tulsa World*.)

During the winter of 1991–92, the Drillers added over two million dollars of expansion and improvements to the stadium. Brian Carroll, director of media relations, holds an architect's model of the new entrance.

The 1992 Drillers roster featured three former Tulsa high school players. Pictured from left to right are Jackson Todd, Kurt Miller, and Paul Postier. Todd pitched at Will Rogers High School. He pitched from 1977–1981 in the majors and coached 11 seasons in the minors, including 1992–1995 as the pitching coach with the Drillers. Miller, a pitcher from Union High School, won seven games for the Drillers in 1992 and played in the majors in the late '90s with the Marlins and the Cubs. Paul Postier was an infielder from Edison High School. He played for the Drillers in 1988–90 and in 1992.

The first nine-inning no-hit game in Drillers Stadium history was a combined effort by three Driller pitchers. On April 18, 1991, starter Cedric Shaw (center) went the first seven innings. He allowed six walks, but picked three of those runners off base. Relievers Everett Cunningham (right) and Barry Manuel (left) pitched the eighth and ninth innings. Tulsa beat Arkansas 2-0. Manuel saved 25 games in 1991 to lead the Texas League. He was the first pitcher in Tulsa history to lead the league in saves.

Robb Nen pitched for Tulsa in parts of the 1990–92 campaigns as a starter. His record as a Driller of 2-9 and no saves did not indicate that he would become one of the top relief pitchers in baseball, saving 314 games in 10 seasons in the major leagues. As 2003 opens, he continues to pitch for the San Francisco Giants.

Trey McCoy was a power hitting first baseman/designated hitter for Tulsa from 1991–93. He hit 41 homers and drove in 133 runs in 184 Driller games. His best season was in 1993 when he led the Texas League with 29 home runs and 95 RBIs while batting .293.

Rick Helling won 12 games for Tulsa in 1993 striking out a league high 188 batters, fourth highest in Tulsa baseball history. He was the first Tulsan to lead a league in strikeouts since Larry Jaster in 1965. Helling has pitched 9 seasons in the major leagues winning 82 games with 896 strikeouts.

In 1990 Tulsa County Stadium was renamed to its current name of Drillers Stadium. The artificial turf was removed and natural grass installed in 1993. The largest regular season crowd in the history of Tulsa baseball was played here on April 8, 1994 as 16,780 saw Tulsa defeat Jackson 6-3. Seating was expanded again in 1995 to its current capacity of 11,009, making it the 15th largest minor league stadium in the country.

The Texas League player of the year for 1996 was Driller first baseman Bubba Smith. Smith stood six foot two inches tall and weighed 230 pounds. He was a very popular player with the fans, leading the league in home runs with 32 and RBIs with 94. He was second in extra base hits, third in hits, and third in slugging percentage.

Outfielder Dan Collier won the 1997 Texas League home run championship with 26. Collier tied the all-time minor league record with a homer in his seventh consecutive game on June 19, 1997.

Also on June 19, 1997 Fernando Tatis, the Driller third baseman, hit three home runs in the same game. He was the first Tulsa player to hit three home runs in a game since Hector Cruz in 1975. It was also the first time a Tulsa player hit three home runs in a game at Drillers Stadium.

Ruben Mateo established the all-time Tulsa record with a 27 game hitting streak from June 16–July 14, 1998. The outfielder hit .309 with 134 hits in 109 games. Mateo has been in the major leagues for the past four seasons, with Texas and Cincinnati.

Jason Conti was a valuable member of the 1998 Texas League champion Drillers. He was the property of the new expansion Arizona Diamondbacks. Conti, a left-handed hitting outfielder, led the Texas League and all of minor league baseball in 1998 with 125 runs scored. Conti's 125 runs was the most by a Tulsa player since John Stoneham scored 138 in 1932. He also led Texas League outfielders with 20 assists. Conti has played in the major leagues the past four seasons with Arizona and Tampa Bay.

Mike Lamb was the offensive leader of the 1999 team that went to the Texas League finals. Playing third base he led the league in hits with 176 and doubles with 51. Both totals were the highest for a Tulsa player since Walt Williams' smashing 1966 season. Lamb has played for the Texas Rangers the last three seasons.

Craig Monroe enjoyed a fine 2000 season for the Drillers. Monroe hit .282 with 20 home runs and scored 89 runs and drove in 89. He led the Texas League outfielders in assists and double plays. On April 8, Monroe tied an all-time Tulsa record with three home runs in a game and nine runs batted in. At that date he was only the second Driller and third player overall to hit three home runs in a single game in Driller Stadium history. His nine RBIs tied the all-time Tulsa baseball record for most RBIs in a single game. Wally Post drove in nine for the Tulsa Oilers in 1950. The RBI mark broke the Drillers Stadium record of seven, set in 1993 by Trey McCoy. Monroe played in the major leagues with Texas and Detroit in 2001 and 2002.

Carlos Pena was a standout on the 2000 team. He hit .299 with 158 hits in 138 games, 28 home runs, a league leading 117 runs, and 105 runs batted in. His RBI total was the highest since Hector Cruz hit 116 in 1975 and was the second highest total for a Tulsa first baseman. Only Joe Adcock in 1949 had more with 116. Pena also tied the all-time Tulsa record with three grand slam homers in a season. Ed Kurpiel also had three in 1974. Pena was on the Detroit Tigers roster as the 2003 season opened.

Bobby Jones has managed more games (1,020) and won more games (496) than anyone else in Tulsa baseball history. Jones played nine seasons in the major leagues as an outfielder and first baseman with Texas and California from 1974–1986. He was a player-coach for the Drillers in 1987, hitting .303. He managed Texas' Single A team from 1988–90. Jones then managed the Drillers in 1991 and 1992, reaching the 1992 playoffs. The Rangers moved him to Triple A Oklahoma City for the 1993–94 campaigns. Jones returned to Tulsa for six more seasons 1995–2000, guiding the Drillers to the 1998 Texas League Championship. The Rangers called Jones up to the major league dugout as a first base/outfield coach in May of 2000. Jones' career win total puts him in the top 10 for wins in Texas League history. Jones was a coach for the Rangers in 2000 and 2001. In 2003 he will be the manager of the Triple A Oklahoma City team.

Hank Blalock became the only player in minor league history to hit for the cycle twice in the same season. In fact, he did it in the same week! On June 26, 2001 the third baseman hit for the cycle at Drillers Stadium. He was the first player to accomplish this feat in Drillers Stadium. history. Two days later, the score was tied in the 11th inning when the game was delayed by rain for an hour. Blalock had a four-for-four night going with a single, two doubles a walk and a triple. When the game resumed, Blalock hit a two-run home run to make history. (Photo Courtesy of *The Tulsa World.*)

Blalock was named the Texas Rangers' minor league player of the year in 2001. He hit .327 at Tulsa and .380 at Single A Charlotte. For the season Blalock had 179 hits and 108 RBIs in 121 games. He split the 2002 season between Texas and Triple A. He was on the Rangers' 40 man roster as the 2003 spring training began. (Photo from 2002 Upper Deck minor league card.)

Mark Teixeira made it two years in a row for a Driller to win the Texas Ranger minor league player of the year award. The third baseman suffered an elbow injury during spring training and it slowed his start in his first pro season. Teixeira hit .316 in 48 games for Tulsa in 2002 with 10 home runs and 28 RBIs, helping the Drillers to the Texas League championship series. On the season, Teixeira played in a combined 86 games for Charlotte and Tulsa with 102 hits and 69 RBIs.

Bruce Howard (right) and Mark Neely have been the popular radio play-by-play voices of the Drillers for 15 summers. Howard began with Tulsa in the 1989 season. In 1995 he became the Director of Broadcasting for the University of Tulsa, announcing the Golden Hurricane football and basketball games. He now fills in on radio broadcasts when Mark Neely announces the Drillers' television games. Howard was honored by his peers in the Tulsa media industry with the Tulsa Sportscaster of the Year award in 1992. Howard is seen above interviewing Hall of Famer Harmon Killebrew.

Mark Neely succeeded Howard in 1996 as the voice of the Tulsa Drillers. Neely broadcasts about 200 live events a year. He also announces high school football and University of Tulsa women's basketball. Neely has won the Tulsa Sportscaster of the Year Award in 1999 and 2002. he has also announced major league games for ESPN.

Tulsa baseball has always had a great relationship with the Tulsa World newspaper. John A. Ferguson (seated) was the baseball beat writer for the World from 1964–1995. Even after he was "semi-retired," Fergy still covered about 10 games a year. The Drillers Stadium press box is named in his honor.

Barry Lewis (left) became the baseball beat writer in 1996. He also covered the Drillers in 1990–1992 for the *Tulsa Tribune* newspaper. A very knowledgeable sportsman, Lewis also is the beat writer for the Tulsa Oiler hockey team. John Klein (standing, center) is the *Tulsa World* sports editor. His baseball background includes being named the college baseball writer for the decade of the 1980s. He wrote the first cover story for *Baseball America*. He also covered the Houston Astros when he was a writer for a Houston newspaper.

TM

Tulsa was affiliated with Texas from 1977 through the 2002 season. The Drillers had an excellent working relationship in those years with the Rangers. However, a new owner took control of the Rangers and in 2000, Texas' ownership decided to own their own Double A franchise. The Rangers built a stadium in Frisco, Texas (about 25 miles away from the Ballpark in Arlington), and purchased the Shreveport team. Although the Drillers were slated to remain with the Rangers through the 2004 season, Tulsa permitted the Rangers to end their affiliation two years early. The Shreveport franchise was transferred to Frisco in September 2002. The Drillers then signed a two-year player development contract with the Colorado Rockies.

One baseball century is behind us. A new one has just begun. What new heroes will emerge to strengthen Tulsa's position as one of the elite baseball cities in America?

Printed in the USA
CPSIA information can be obtained
at www.ICGtesting.com
LVHW070756241223
767241LV00009B/895